THE WHITE STAR OF THE EAST

THE GREAT AWAKENING

Volume VIII

A series of superbly informative and prophetic messages,
downloaded and transcribed originally as newsletters by

Sister Thedra

These precious messages are reprinted herein.

ISBN: 978-1-7363418-2-7

Contents

Mission Statement

Give the truth to the world. Let it be received where it will. Many will read the messages. Some will accept the truth, others will read through curiosity, a few will ridicule. Yet to all is the truth given, and to all remains the power of choice.

The hope of the world in these times is in spiritualizing all forms of activity---promoting understanding through love and service. These must be the watchwords if the world is to come into lasting peace. We are trying to influence a world that is going astray and could cause undreamed of suffering. We are trying to overcome the thought of materialists and to bring a spiritual outlook into the earthly life. We need the help of all on earth who can think in spiritual terms. The great battle to be fought now is between the spiritual and the material, between idealism and carnalism. You can help by spreading the word---we are asking that you help because the battle may be long and the victory far away.

Halls of Light is not allied with any sect, denomination, political entity, organization, neither endorses nor opposes any cause. There are no dues for membership. Halls of Light is self-supporting through its own voluntary contributions. Halls of Light has but one purpose: to help through encouragement and understanding...

To contact the publishers or to obtain copies of our other books, please contact us at email: goldtown11@gmail.com

Esu Jesus Sananda

This reproduction is from an actual photograph taken on June 1st, 1961, in Chichen Itza, Yucatan, by one of thirty archaeologists working in the area at the time. Sananda appeared in visible, tangible body and permitted His photograph to be taken.

About the Late Sister Thedra

> Since the later part of the last Century the Kumara
> wisdom preserved by Aramu Muru has begun to reemerge
> into the world. This process began with the late Sister
> Thedra, whom Jesus Christ appeared physically to while
> on her deathbed and spontaneously healed her of cancer
> while she was in the Yucatan, where she had gone to
> accept her fate, and the will of our Lord Jesus Christ.
> That is when something miraculous occurred.
> --sus spoke to her saying, "My name is Esu Sananda
> Kumara" and then sent Thedra down to the Monastery of
> the Seven Rays to learn the Kumara wisdom.
> After five years, Thedra was told to return to the
> United States where she founded the Association of
> Sananda and Sanat Kumara at Mt. Shasta in California.
> While heading this organization, Thedra channeled many
> messages from Sananda and taught the Kumara wisdom
> until her passing in 1992.
> While in the Yucatan It is said that while Sister
> during the 1960s Thedra was in the Yucatan, she was
> told a se-ret by her friend George Hunt Williamson,
> also known as Brother Philip, who authored Secrets of
> the Andes, and the SECRET PLACES OF THE LION.
> Williamson, confided in his long-time friend Sister
> Thedra that he intentionally scrambled the
> reincarnational lineages in order to protect this next
> generation when they the Mayan Solar Priests, who were
> the direct line descendants of the Kumara according to

> prophesy were scheduled to reincarnate or return to
> fulfill their missions upon Earth, one of which was to
> relocate these ancient sites where the original records
> of the Amaru were placed for safe keeping.
> Sister Thedra, 1900-1992, spent five years at the abbey
> undergoing intensive spiritual training and > initiations.
> While in South America in the Yucatan, she had an
> experience which changed her in an instant when as it
> is told by her that Jesus Christ physically appeared to
> her and spontaneously cured her of cancer.
>
> He introduced himself to her by his true, name,
> "Sananda Kumara," thereby revealing his affiliation
> with the Venusian founders of the Great Solar
> Brotherhoods. It was by his command that Sister Thedra
> went to Peru where in here travels she met Williamson.
> Sister Thedra eventually left Peru upon telling her
>experience there was complete.
> Even before she returned to the States she met with
> harsh criticism from the church, which she elected to
> leave. (JW That was the church that is in Salt Lake
> City, Utah.)
> She then traveled to Mt. Shasta in California and
> founded the Association of Sananda and Sanat Kumara.
> A.S.S.K.
>
> You ask, Is There A Difference Between Jesus and
> Sananda?
> Our Lords name given at birth by his father Joseph, and
> his beloved mother Mary was Yeshua, thus being of the

> house of David and the order of Yoseph, he would be
> called Yeshua ben Yoseph.
>
> The Roman Emperors placed the name of Jesus upon the
> sir name of Yeshua, after the Emperor Justinian adopted
> Christianity as the official faith of Rome, and ordered
> that the sacred books be compiled, upon approval of a
> specially appointed council, appointed by the Emperor,
> into a recognizable and uniform work titled The Bible.
> Prior to this there never was a Bible per se.
>
> There existed until the time of the Emperor's edict, a
> selection of many Sacred texts, that were employed in
> the Sacred Teachings. Many of which were copies of
> what the Greeks had transposed from the original texts
> in the Libraries of Alexandria, which were originally
> compiled by Alexander the Great, and were destroyed by
> Julius Caesar, fearing that they might prove dangerous
> to the rule of a Caesar, an Earthly God.
> In addition, it kept. (he thought) the knowledge of
> Alexander's Libraries, out of the hands of the
> Ptolemy's, who were said to be descended from his
> bloodline.
> At the time Caesar had no way of knowing the vast
> portions of the Library that were already in the
> Americas, in the Great Universities of the Inca, and
> the Maya.
> Yeshua spent many years in the East after his
> ascension.
> The good Sheppard, upon his appearances to the

> Apostles after his ascension told his Apostles that he
> was in fact going to tend to his Father's other sheep;
> which means, plainly that he was continuing upon his
> sacred journey.
> As the ascended one, Yeshua took to himself the name of
> Sananda, meaning the Christed one, and Sananda was
> thus embraced forever more by the Great Solar
> Brotherhood.
> To many of you this is all new, to others it will be
> received as a welcome easing of the wall that has so
> long separated two sides of the same coin, this is
> being placed into the ethers and the matrix of thought
> at this time as it is the time of the Awakening, and
> the Christos is already emerging into the new
> consciousness, and mother Earth herself.
>
> Sister Thedra and the phenomenon of channeling.
> Authority to use the name of Sananda was given to
> Sister Thedra when Jesus~ Sananda appeared to her in the
> Yucatan, and cured her instantly of the cancer that had
> taken her body over.
> Further, he allowed a picture of his continence to be
> taken at that time that she might realize the
> occurrence was more than a dream. (JW I was told by
> my teacher and Guru Merelle Fagot that Thedra had
> a large format camera called a 620, if I remember right,
> and it had bellows on it and founded out. She used
> this to take the picture of Sananda. Merele said that
> she got some real good pictures with that camera. I
> have seen this picture that Thedra took and Sananda

> didn't look very handsome, he just looked like a normal
> person with not too long of hair and he had very dark
> skin.)
> Sanada's Message to her by Sister Thedra.
> "Sori Sori: Mine hand I have placed upon thine head,
> and I have given unto thee the authority to use Mine
> name. Give unto them the name Sananda, by which they
> shall know Me as the Lord thy God - the Son of God, sent
> that ye be made to know me, the One sent from out the
> inner temple that there be Light in the world of men."
> (The meaning of "Lord God: "The Lord God, for he is
> "Lord" of, and responsible for, that which he has
> brought forth.)
> "Now it is come when ones which have the will to follow
> Me shall come to know Me by that name which I commanded
> thee to give unto the world as Mine "New name."
> There are many that shall call upon the name of Jesus,
> yet, they will deny the new name as they are want to do.
> While unto thee I give assurance that I am the One sent
> that there be Light in the world of men. Now let this
> be understood, that they that deny Mine New Name deny
> Me by any name. So be it I have appointed thee Mine
> spokesman; I've given unto thee the power and authority
> to speak for being that which I AM. And I say unto thee
> Mine child whom I have called forth and anointed thee
> with the Holy Spirit, thy name shall be as it is now
> called, Thedra - that name I spoke unto thee from out
> the ethers, and thou heard Me and accepted that which I
> gave unto thee; and wherein have I deceived thee?
> Wherein have I forgotten thee, or left thee alone?"

> "I say unto thee, Mine hand is upon thee and I shall
> sustain thee and you shall come to know that which I
> have kept for thee. So be it that I have kept thy
> reward, and at no time shall it be dissipated of
> scattered, for it is intact. So let this Mine Word
> suffice them which question thee - let them question,
> and I shall bear witness for thee. For do I not know
  Mine servants from the traitor?
> Do I not reward Mine servants according unto their
> works or merits? I speak that they might know that I am
> mindful of Mine servants, that I am not a poor puny
> priest who has forgotten his servants."
>
> "I say unto them, Mine servants shall be glorified
> above the crowned heads of the nations which have set
> themselves apart, and denied Me Mine part of Mine word
> for they have turned from Me in their conceit and
> forgetfulness."
> "Now let this go on record as Mine Word, and I shall
> give unto them proof, which are of a mind to follow Me.
> So be it as I have spoken and I am not finished; I
> shall speak again and again, and I shall rise Mine
> Voice against them which set foot against Mine
> servants, and they shall be as ones cast out. So let
> them ask of Me and I shall enlighten them. So be it I
> know where of I speak. Be ye as ones blest to accept Me
> and know Me for that which I AM.
> The Final Messages >
. On Saturday, June 13, 1992, at exactly 10.00 PM, at the age of
92,

> Sister Thedra made her final transition from the comfort of her
own bed. When the time
> arrived, she simply took one small breath and slipped
> quietly away, without pomp or fanfare.
> She left as she had lived...as a humble servant for the
> greater good.
> The messages that follow were given to Sister Thedra
> shortly before her transition.
> They are compiled here to give you some idea of the
> significance of her passing and of the expansion of the
> work, as she is now free to work unencumbered by the
> physical limitations and by the pain which has so
> encumbered her in the past.
> She has carried on the work here on the Earth plane for
> the last 50 years because that's where the work was
> needed...rest assured that her work now in the higher
> realms will simply be an extension of that work.

Sananda's Appearance

Be ye as one which hast heard Mine Voice and responded unto it - for I speak that ye hear, and I say that which is wise and prudent.

Let it be known that I, the Lord thy God hast spoken and bear ye witness of Me, for I have made manifest Mineself that ye might know Me - and for this wast these manifestations made.

I say I have made Mineself manifest that ye might see Me with thine mortal eyes; that ye might bear witness of Me. Yet thine companions saw and believed not; neither did they hear, for they were selfish and unprepared - yet did I deny them?

I say; I came that they which would might see and hear. I went and came again unto Mine own. So be it that I have found; I have given unto the found that they which know not might KNOW; that they might come to know as thou knowest.

Yet, how many hast turned from Me and persecuted thee for Mine Word. It is said, "Woe unto them which persecute Mine servants." Is it not the law which they set into motion?

Yea, Mine beloved, I say they bring about their own downfall. So be it that I am a compassionate one, and I would that they know what they do. So be it they shall learn well their lessons. So let it be, for this is the mercy of God, the One which hast sent me.

So be it I AM the wayshower, the Lord thy God.

I AM Sananda

THE WHITE STAR OF THE EAST

Part I

Sori Sori: This is the beginning of a part which shall be new unto thee, and it shall be prepared for the populace in a very short while. This part shall be as the whole of one book with no commonalities, for the subject matter shall be different from any other. While it shall be finished after ye have returned from the place wherein ye shall go with the book (Mine Intercom Messages), after which ye shall go unto the place which is designated unto thee as "The School". This shall be after thine return from The School and ye shall release such information as is necessary, as none other hast been privy too. So be ye as one prepared, for there are great things in store for thee. So be it and Selah.

* * * * *

Sori Sori: Ye shall be as one to bring forth this news/information as it has never been given before. The information is of great concern unto us of our realm. When this information is released there shall be a wave of confusion and disbelief... yet there shall be great relief for the ones which have asked for light - <u>The truth seekers</u>.

It is now come when it is expedient to release such information, it is part of the work of our school. For this shall it be seen and understood that we, the Host, are not playing second place unto any man of planet Earth. It is now come when such material shall be made available, yet not many are prepared to be mine messenger or

1

scribe. This work of getting these portions out unto the ones which are seeking truth (naught else), is no small task.

While it is given unto few, in comparance with the populace, to ask for this truth which is now available, the populace, or major part of the people of Earth, will have none of it.... reject it as fantasy. Yet it is foreseen that many shall embrace this truth and give unto 'us', the Host, credit for bringing it forth that they be enlightened, for these have waited long for such enlightenment. They shall know the truth of such information, and accept it with joy and thanksgiving.

For this it is given unto thee to be prepared to go forth with such as we shall give unto thee for them. While there shall be the bigots... the traitors... the foolish, unlearned... that shall deny thee and bring great stress upon the ones which accept such truth as is brought forth for their sake, one and all... unto the traitors which reject such truth/information, I say, it is for thine good that "we" come in love and fulfillment of the law. It is for thine own good that we labor without ceasing or so called recompense. It is for our love that we come into the darkness of thine world that there be light, that ye be as one enlightened, free from thine bonds of unknowing, the ignorance which is bondage.

Yea, bondage it is. When ye have been presented with such materials as we are prepared to release, it behooves thee to consider well its worth/value and be as ones willing to learn. To lay aside thine preconceived ideas and opinions, to weigh, consider the value of it, unbiased by that which hast been unto thee thine legirons.

Give unto me credit for being that which I am and I shall prove mineself. I am not a traitor. I am come of mine Father. He hast sent

2

me that ye might return unto him with me. I am one of the Host which I have brought with me for the purpose of bringing thee out before the great day of sorrow and suffering. <u>This</u> is our <u>intent</u>, our mission at this time.

Be ye as one to open wide thine sleepy eyes, that ye see clearly that which is new unto thee. For each and every day is new unto the ones which have eyes to see clearly that which is new unto thee. For each and every day is now unto the ones which have eyes to see... the ones which have a will to learn.

None other shall move into the "Age of Light," for they shall be as ones which <u>have not the will</u> to learn of me, as one with the mighty Host. What a host it is!!

We have come as the Lighted Ones, sent of our Father which ye have not remembered in thine days or sojourn within the realm of darkness, which has been thine lot for lo the eons. Now the time is come when ye shall be as ones prepared to receive thine freedom, and there shall be great light within thee which shall lift thee into the realm in which we exist... wherein is no darkness... no sorrow. Be it such as we bring unto thee, present unto thee, this day.

Shall ye give unto me/us credit for being that which we claim to be? Or, shall ye deny thine inheritance and forfeit thine eternal freedom. Ye have been given the gift of freewill. None bring thee against thine will, it is not lawful... we dare not... indeed, it would be an impossibility.

* * * * *

The King Of Glory

Sori Sori: There is one by the name of Marshula, which is desirous of speaking with thee. For this is his desire and I have given unto him passport. Receive him in mine name.

ᕯᕯᕯ : Greetings mine sister of light. Be ye blest to receive of me, for I come as 'One Sent'.

The time is come when we, you and I, shall have a part to play in the "Greatest Show on Earth". So be it that we have been part of other 'shows' in ages long past. Now once again we are called forth of the Mighty Council to add our parts unto this present one, which shall be the final and greatest of all.

So be it that there shall appear within the heavens, the sign which heralds the opening of this one in which we shall be participants. For this we shall be as one with the mighty Host, which is the Christ Council and the guardians which have been within the realms of light prepared for this day.

This is the greatest day that hast ever, in the time of Earths existence, been brought forth through and by the will of the Father Mother God. This is the "Day of Deliverance" from bondage for Mother Earth and her children, when ye shall declare thine self free... free... free... Free At Last! ye shall know that which is thine part. That which ye have played in the time past, the eons long past, shall be as the open book which is not of Earth only, yet it is not as one recorded by human hand. It is as recorded within the firmaments. The stars bear witness of these events, therefore no mistakes are made in the recording of such events.

By the hand of the Father hast these recordings been set as perfect time records for the Council of Light. All things which are past and future are recorded within these records, which shall be opened unto the ones which are so prepared to read.

So be it that there is a plan which is perfect now within its place, active and effective with the lives of each and every one (being) within the universe. Not one shall be left out, for the 'perfect plan' includes all life forms.

When the White Star of the East appears within the heavens, it is the herald of the coming. The coming of the new day, the coming of the King of Glory to claim his own, to take his Kingdom.

* * * * *

Sori Sori: Be ye glad this day is come, for it is given unto me to say that there are signs in the heavens which betokens mans awakening. O, glorious day! For long have we, thy Guardians, waited and watched the struggles of mankind in his darkness and illusions. His dreams hast been as horrorful nightmares which hast been as chains about his neck.

For this have we of the Host of Light drawn nigh, for we see that his deliverance is nigh. The firmaments of the heavens declare it so, so shall it be.

Let thine hearts be full of joy! Lift up thine eyes and see the signs, and behold the glory of God the Father, for he hast sent his sons in great light and love. He hast been as the Creator Father, sending forth his Creator Sons to do his bidding. He has spoken the Word and the firmaments of the heavens have moved to his words, as in unison unto his command. Not one star of the heavens shall be out of place, for all is in order.

Now it is said: There shall be great changes upon the earth, and quickly shall they come!

O, man of Earth, could ye but see the glory of the great and grand plan, ye would rejoice with us. Ye would know as we know, that there is but life eternal, and everlasting power of light which holds the firmaments within place.

This is the day long foretold, while ye, man of Earth, hast groveled within the Earth for a pittance in thine unknowing and confusion. This is our mission, to set thee free, and all which will it so shall arise and come forth as of the Light... they shall be free.

It is said; "Seek ye the light, and all things of light shall be added." Have ye understood the fullness of this message? I say, nay! ye have not. For this, are we of the Host come that there be understanding. We come in unison, as one body, one mind, one purpose, that ye, man, be lifted out of the pit of darkness, of ignorance of that which is going on round and about thee while ye have wallowed in thine filth and deceit. Thine own undoing comes not from above... it is thine own rebellion!

Now it is said: Come ye forth, humbly seeking the light which is the substance of all that is created "good", which is permanent. Light is the substance of spirit. Know ye what spirit is? What life is? Eternal it is.

Hast thou not wearied of thine forgetfulness... thine slothfulness... thine unknowing? Hast thou not asked for release? It is now made possible by the love and power invested within us, the Mighty Council.

Behold ye the Light, and praise ye the Father which is Light, that which is thine/our source of being. Let it be the day for which we have waited.

It shall bear fruit!

Amen and Selah

* * * * *

Sori Sori: Say I unto thee this day; there are ones which are ready to receive thee and be as ones to minister unto thee. For it is given unto me to know thee as one which hast been as one prepared for the "Greater Part." So be it ye shall come into the place wherein I am as one which hast given of thineself without thought of recompence. Ye have gone the long way with me.

This is mine time, and I shall speak as one knowingly, and as one in authority. I am come that ye might have thine freedom from bondage. This is of great concern unto us of the Host, for we see and know that which hast been accomplished by thine effort, as one called out from among them. Ye have walked as one sober, never flinching or looking back. Now I say unto thee, ye shall see as we of the Host, that which hast been accomplished by thine own work and effort while ye have walked as one not knowing that which is being accomplished by or through thine labors.

Now it is come when ye shall walk as I, knowingly, and see as I see. And there shall be the harvest reaped and the joy shall be great, for we of the Host shall be as thy host, and ye shall be as one of us.

And there shall be the 'gathering in' which shall be as one bound in love, for one part, one purpose. The cycle shall be completed and ye shall no more go into bondage. NO MORE shall ye go into darkness as one bound, for it is <u>finished</u>.

I say ye shall be free, even as we of the host are free, and ye shall know the meaning of freedom. So be it a joyful reunion.

A great day shall it be for it is finished, the part ye have played, as one sent into the world of man, unknowingly of that which ye encountered on the 'long and weary journey.' Ye have given freely and lovingly of thine energy, without crying out or going back into despair or rebellion.

It is now the time of reaping. Ye shall see as we see, for it shall be shown unto thee as it is recorded upon thine record(s) which are preserved. Yea, even for thine own eyes hast it been preserved, for at no time hast thou been alone. No, not one moment hast thou walked alone. It is for this that we hast walked with thee that ye might have the way made straight before thee, and safe. For there hast been times of great danger and heavy burdens which we have seen and shared with thee.

Now hast come the hour of sharing the joy which comes when one is finished his mission and comes unto us, as one prepared to become one with us. O, the joy of such freedom... release from bonds that bind the poor unknowing neophyte. Yet, he holds fast unto the memory within his soul, which hast been his sustainer...

which is our part to hold and guide, sustain the light within. For this we give our love and light.

Be ye as one which hast come with the awareness of thine oneness with us thine benefactors, thine brothers. Equal art we, and we share such joy as ye shall know. This is mine joy, to speak at this hour, for thine hour swiftly approaches.

Be ye as one with us, for it is so according unto the Law, that thine time is come when ye shall sing the glad anthem with us... Welcome Home.

I Am thine brother and thine host. Be ye as one enlightened and give thanks with us, as one with us, for art thou not one of us?

So let it be a joyful homecoming.

* * * * *

Sori Sori: This is mine word for thee this day. There shall be a place in which ye shall go which shall accept thee as one of them. These shall be enlightened ones which shall know thee and thine works. There shall be a feasting and gladness.

Be ye as one prepared, for it shall be the beginning of a new part for thee, which shall be of great light and vast knowledge, which shall be for the good of all. Many shall profit from this, thine new part, so be it and Selah.

This shall be as the beginning of this said new part, which is now begun. Be ye not concerned for that which ye know not, for it is of no concern unto thee at this moment... all shall be revealed as is necessary. Be ye prepared to go when called, which shall be at the right/proper time. No mistake is allowed in this our part or place, for we are at our stations in readiness for action... be it that which it may.

For this do we give unto thee this word; be ye as one prepared to answer our call. Fret not for foolish things... give unto me thine attention. There is one which is prepared to come in full armor, to bring thee into this place wherein I Am. He shall be as one which shall sponsor thee and be unto thee "host." Let it be a glad time for there shall be many which shall receive thee with love and recognition. Ye shall be appraised of that which ye shall do aforehand, so be ye at peace, and rest thine physical body.

* * * * *

Sori Sori: While it is nigh time for thine coming unto us of the school which we have been speaking of, ye have not envisioned such as ye shall encounter. As ye enter herein ye shall be greeted with great joy. And preparation shall be in evidence, for ye shall be awed by/with the great beauty and simplicity of that which is evident... the evidence of our joy and regard for thee and thine cooperation. This is as a small part of that which ye shall experience in thine time of being within this place wherein we are.

There shall be another place wherein ye shall go for greater learning, which shall be for thine greater part. So be it that ye shall be as one made aware of things ye have not imagined nor dreamed possible. Yet, ye shall know that which shall be great revelation that shall be unto mankind as helpful unto him in his progress and ascension from darkness into light. This is the part which shall be part of thine greater part.

So be it we of the host shall be as <u>One</u> on which/whom ye shall rely for accurate information. There shall be nothing hidden or withheld, for it is come when ye shall come into the fullness of thine inheritance.

So be it that I/we shall speak unto thee yet again on the subject of this place wherein ye shall come as one prepared.

* * * * *

MASADA

Sori Sori: It is I which hast called thee; ye hast heard mine call and answered me. Let us be as one in this project, which shall be as great light on an old subject.

There were ones, in times past of many centuries, which dwelt within the land called the 'Holy Land'. This part of the planet Earth dwelt in darkness of great proportions. The wickedness and superstition was prevailing among most of the people. There was little understanding among the ones which dared to set themselves up as teachers of truth and wisdom. These ones which so did, gave, in the most part, of their own unknowing and superstition. They which were learned of the Holy Spirit were called fools or heretics... some were put to death by many torturous means. The history written by the generations that followed these days of slaughter and degradation, was as biased; translated and put through many changes to fit the beliefs and conform to the like of the recorders, the priests and teachers, many of which composed the 'judges and jury' which perpetuated the slaughter of the people which held steadfast unto their beliefs/customs.

Now it is come when I am prepared to bring forth the truth of many records which have been distorted and handed down as truth, even unto this present day! I am of a humor to set straight some of these records which are of great import unto many which now sit in council with me, as ones of truth and justice. This is but the pre-amble. There is much to come forth for to set straight the record for any and all which are seeking truth.

12

I have access unto the imperishable records, therefore, I shall reveal unto mine tried and true handmaiden this record as it is so written on the akasia. For this! shall be lenient with her, and there shall be no stress, pain, or doubt, for I have prepared this one for this portion which I shall call the "Masada", which shall be as truth and light unto a misled and wayward/backward people (of the 'Holy Land'). These which have not known the true from the false.

There are two peoples, divided one in front, one behind. I did not say; one on my right, one on my left, for neither ones are with me, for they are not of mine ones which serve me, sent of the Father God... the giver of life and mercy... love.

I am sent of the Father God, which is light, love and mercy. He it is which hast given unto all mankind to walk upright, breathe and have their being upon the planet Earth.

Now it is come, as the seasons come and go through the centuries, that it is seen that there are these ones from centuries past, which are returned unto the place which hast been as the spawning ground of these infamous crimes committed against each other in the name of religion, each differing one from the other. Yea, many names have they called their gods. Yea, they have made gods of their warriors and worshiped them! These are as the ones which have the black cape over their eyes... they see not that which they do. They walk in darkness; they fear the Light; they deny the truth which I brought, which I have given forth from the realm of light. For it is given unto these ones the dark side of life, which they claim unto themself as being the only way unto salvation; while they murder/slaughter their fellow man for a puny penny... a counterfeit coin which shall melt within their hand.

Now, the time is at hand that these ones, without one discounted, shall be brought up short. Their time shall end, for long have they held sway within the dark places wherein they work their plans of pillage and carnage. It shall be brought to a sudden halt, for they have so brought it to be. <u>Not as they have imaged</u>, for they have not reckoned with the law given unto them in the beginning. They have set themselves up and made laws to suit themself, each unto his own. Yea, they have fashioned great temples, mosques, churches, and given bread and wine, (<u>in mine name?</u>), and called it mine body? mine blood? not knowing that which theydo.

What? I ask of them... What think ye do this in mine name? Never was it so. Why dost thou not learn of me before ye make such pompous claims? I tell thee of a surety, ye shall come to nought, for the age of revelation is now come, when truth shall be the cry of the people which are sent upon the planet Earth to clean the ravages of the unknowing hard hearted. For some, the soulless ones, they are ones which have served as the puppets of the dark brothers.

* * * * *

By mine own hand shall I lead thee, and I shall show thee that which I shall give unto thee to do. And ye shall know that which ye do. Ye shall have no rebellion, no fear, for ye shall be part of the 'team' which shall be as a '<u>research</u> team', shall we call it for the sake of making it clear. This part of thine portion which shall be but part of a great and grand record which shall be given out as the <u>true</u> record taken from the akasia.

Be ye as one to know, as ye have been chosen as one with others which have been cleared for this mission. Therein shall be no

14

mistakes, no more distortion of facts, no fear, for I shall lead the way before thee.

* * * * *

Sori Sori: This day ye shall gather together and give unto them these words, for it is expedient that they know that which I say unto thee:

There shall be called to gather, a council, within the place wherein | abide, to decide that which shall be done with the Middle East situation. When we have gone the last mile with them and they relent not unto our suggestions/propositions, we are under orders to let them bring an end unto themself. This is not our choice, yet it is necessary that this be done in the shortest of time, as ye know time.

It hast been written, while not in detail, it is seen from our vantage point that it be the way in which it shall bring about the least carnage. Be ye alert and fear not, for it is the way these foolish children have chosen. Its not our will, neither our choice. Know ye that they have given of their energy that they be destroyed.

When it is come that the warriors have brought about their own destruction, there shall be a great change upon the Earth and its people, as they shall see the foolishness of their way. It is foreseen that which hast been the misuse of energy, which hast been the reaping, the harvest of their sowing, the rebounding of the law.

Be ye as the one to watch with diligence. Know ye the law... respect it and be as one prepared to look upon thine own record and judge thine own actions. See that which ye have sown, for surely ye shall reap as ye have sown. Know ye that which ye have buried within the past shall be revealed within the present, for this is the day of examination, the day of accounting. So let it be as it is written.

* * * * *

There shall be a loud voice which shall be heard about the land, and that voice shall proclaim the truth of mine words. No man shall say he did not hear, for it is foretold that each shall hear in his own tongue.

And it is foreseen that some shall run to hide. They shall find no hiding place, for there shall be no place wherein to cover themself. Even the foxes shall not find their holes.

Sori Sori: This day I shall speak of the day to come when ye shall depart from the Gatehouse. There shall be a place wherein ye shall go for a time, therein ye shall learn many things which are new unto thee. For this there is great preparation.

It shall be given unto thee to learn much which shall be given forth unto the people which are unaware of such as ye shall give unto them. Ye shall be as one prepared for that which ye shall bring forth for the good of all.

This part shall be as none yet given unto the populace, for it is written and truly so that I shall do a new thing, and there shall be a great stir and much talk, while there shall be little understanding. Yet it shall burst forth as a great light upon the people, for I shall send mine ambassadors forth among them that they might awaken. For the time swiftly approaches when it shall be necessary that they know that which shall be brought forth.

16

They which hear shall know that which they hear. The ones which see shall know that which they see. They shall have the understanding of that which is being given unto them for the good of all.

Let it be understood that there are great changes which shall be made manifest, both within the world of form and within the spirit of man. It shall be according unto the law of the cosmos. The cycle of the past, which is <u>now past</u>, brings <u>great new changes</u> which hast not been conceived by man of Earth. The new shall be as a light unto their feet... an awakening which shall be unto them their freedom from ALL bondage. And such as hast been given unto them within the past shall be as the dark age, for they shall have the understanding of that which they have been given aforehand was for their growth, while they were without the understanding of that which was to follow. They, <u>mankind</u> of the past, hast for the greater part, worked unknowingly of that which was to come from their labors of this day.

* * * * *

Sori Sori: This is a day of rejoicing, for it is come when ye shall begin thine journey towards the place wherein ye shall be as one received into the school, wherein ye shall be as one which hast been prepared for entrance. There be but a short journey, indeed, a short time.

Now it is come that ye shall see as with new eyes, walk as with new legs, and ye shall not fall. Be ye as one which hast mine hand upon thee, for I am with thee unto the end. I shall bear witness of thee, so be it and selah.

* * * * *

Sori Sori: For this hour let us speak of the 'light workers.' Now I ask of thee, who are these which call themself light workers? Know ye these? I say unto thee these which speak so glibly of themself know not that which light is... neither that which is the reflection of light. They but make mock of that which they do not understand.

It is come when they shall see themself as one unknowing, for many things shall be revealed unto them within the next year of your 3rd dimension. They then shall stand as ones in awe of the new understanding, and be as ones humbled by the new found learning. I say be ye as one blest to be prepared to accept the new revelations, for it shall come... IT SHALL COME!.. and all shall be blest which accept it, for it shall be as nothing they/ye have known.

Things are moving across the cosmos which ye have not even dreamed of, which shall change thine Earth, the planet upon which ye dwell... yet it shall be as one with the law of the cosmos.

We, thine benefactors, know for long this day shall be the fulfilling of the prophets, for it is our part to foretell of such things, yet it is not given unto man to understand such as hast been foretold so long ago.

It is written in stone, on parchments, in the skies, yea even into thine cosmogony for anyone so prepared to read. These hast given forth such information for the ones of this day to find and learn. The day hast come when the heavens shall reveal her secrets. So be it the Earth on which ye stand shall give up her secrets and it shall be a time of learning, and great joy shall be upon her, the Earth, for there shall be war no more. So be it and Selah.

* * * * *

Sori Sori: I, Sananda, do proclaim this a day of awakening. This is the beginning of the fulfilling of mine mission which was finished for the "Picean Age".

Now that the Aquarian Age is come, I am returned in full power and wisdom. For this it is given unto me to know the ones which are ready to receive me. These which have kept their covenant with me shall be as ones to go all the way with me. They shall follow where I lead them and thus be prepared to enter into the place of mine abode with me.

So be it that I am come as one which hast the power to go and come as man of Earth, or to be as I am... free to be as pure light with no obstruction, for it is given unto me to know that which is the law of life, which hast no end, and forever is light.

I have been within the places of great learning, which is not of Earth... which are the schools of the Gods of all manifestation... the so-called scientists of all creation manifestation, which can and do bring forth that which is life of the many forms, such as man and his companion, such as the creatures which walk upon four legs, creep upon their belly, and those which fly with wings. These, being Earth mans companions, are under a new law, a new 'dispensation', therefore I am come within the light which hast been revealed unto the ones which have prepared themself for this day.

Now it is come when there shall be great changes amongst and within man of Earth, for the old shall pass away and all things shall be made new. There shall be a great shout of joy go forth from the Earth as she goes into her new birth, delivered of her son which shall be as a moon. Now this hast been spoken of within mine previous book of messages (Mine Intercom Messages from the Realms of Light), therefore I need not repeat in this mine reminder herein. For this I would remind thee that I need no mans counsel or reminder of mine position or post, for I am the son of the living God, sent of him that this new age, that of Aquarius, be the great and joyous area wherein man might fulfill his purpose for which he was created to be.

Let us view the situation of the day from thy present standpoint. There are two people; one stands upon a hill top, one stands in the valley below. The one sees the sun set first, one hast a larger view. Now which one is this? the one on the mountain top or the one in the valley?

So it is with mine children which are going forth in that which is referred to as the 'work.' These which call themself "light workers", which is not as yet understood by the ones which dwell in the valley, in the shadow of the mountain.

Wherein cometh the light? Wherein are the shadows? For this I am come that there be light within this day. It is said there shall be no darkness within mine place of abode, for I am not within the valley; I am on the mountain wherein the sun never sets.

So be it ye shall come to know that which I have caused to be put upon paper as a testimony in the days ahead. By mine own hand have I caused this testimony to be brought forth as proof of mine plan at work in these days of thine own unknowing and waiting. From this day forward one shall see from the highest perspective.

At the present there are few which have the understanding of the part they play in the building of the 'New World' which shall be as nothing they have imaged... neither conceived within their philosophies. It shall be as new within the heaven round and about. The place is prepared to receive this new Earth, this planet, which shall be as one transmuted. For this shall she, the Earth, be called the 'New Earth' truly so. She shall be as new - purified and justified.

She has given of herself that mankind might bring forth many generations which shall be as the guardians of lesser beings, lesser in intelligence, devoid of lessons learned... the ones known as laggards.

These ones, which have given of themself that the younger be brought to maturity, shall be as ones to inherit the New Earth. While the laggards shall be given another place, within the near place wherein the Earth hast fostered her sons as the inheritors of the New Earth.

These ones of great wisdom shall be as the ones which have earned the right to call themself Sons of God, for they have gone out as fledglings which hast proven themself worthy of the trust invested within them. They have walked in the light of the Creator of all that is... All... that one which is the All, the life, the breath... the wholeness of the All, in which we all have our being.

Now it is come when all mystery shall be made clear. No more shall ye stumble over words or illusions, for the illusion shall be no more and light shall be thine part, thine shield and buckler.

Nothing of darkness, fear, and sorrow, shall enter thine being, for ye shall be as one of light, where there are no limits... nothing which bind thee or holds thee fast. The ALL shall be as one vast light which contains such beauty and joy that all things are of one essence which knows that which is... wherein there is no end... no beginning. So be it that this is called the Everness, the ALLness, the "Father".

Now no man dare call himself Father, for man of Earth is but a fragment of the ALL. This is as unknown unto the ones which have the black hood over his eyes.

* * * * *

Sori Sori: Mine word unto thee this hour is: There are ones which have been as the traitors unto themself in past time. They have made for themself great karma which they are now reaping... they are crying and pleading for relief from persecution. These are the ones which were the persecutors of the past age which called themself the "chosen of God"... now they are down-trodden and persecuted.

For this shall they suffer more; the law is precise and just. The persecuted today shall be the oppressor tomorrow... So it goes, as the clock turns. The time for the balancing cometh as surely as the sun rises o'er the hills of the east-land wherein many a generation of warriors have come and gone. Now it is come when it shall be finished. Before another generation hast been brought to maturity, this age shall bring about the balance... karma paid for past sowing.

While the dastardly deeds committed in that balancing shall bring about another age of balancing, for this are the ones which are now the persecutors and the oppressed both in jeopardy. They have gone so far that there is no way they can satisfy the law or claim peace... No justification shall they find. Neither ones shall be as justified, for hatred is so ingrained within their psychic that it shall be another age, upon another plane/place, wherein or upon where they shall find that they are brothers... flesh of one flesh. There they shall learn that love is the only way to "peace". Then the love, one for the other, shall be so established that they shall be as one people, one plan. And that shall be the end of their wars and hatred, and their record shall be as a record balanced within the cosmos.

This is a time of great stress, a time of balancing. Be ye not concerned with where and how it comes about, for that shall not be revealed unto any man of Earth.

That which is now foreseen for these people of the Mid-East is not, as yet, made manifest, as it shall [symbol omitted] with a great speed, a great shout, and much anguish. It shall be as the cleansing, purging of the Earth, of all that hast been deposited within the Earth atoms, (and) the cosmos round about the Earth, which has been the cause of unrest, unpaid karma.

Now the time is at hand when Mother Earth has been given permission to throw these ones off her back. For it is now come when she shall be free to move out into her new port, cleansed of all darkness, and oppression shall not follow in her flight, for the way shall be clear. And for this are we of the light, within the great universe in which we are part, privileged to be positioned to oversee these conditions in so-called time and space. It is with the greatest wisdom and knowledge of the law of life, and its fullness everlasting, eternal, that we are prepared to do that which is given to us to do in each and every situation which entails that of cosmic proportions.

Be ye of Earth not so unknowing as to turn thine head, thine mind, in another direction from that which is given unto thee in this short and simple manner. For the foolish listens unto himself, in his pride and ignorance of that which he knows not. Yea, even unto himself he gives credit for being wise while he goes headlong into destruction.

We are placing before him that which is designed to arouse/awaken him, this man of Earth, which hast been a participant in all that is now being his lot, his part, in the balancing of the law. Each shall bear his part, be it small or large, a day or aeon... none escape the law.

Now, there are many which have parts in this plan which is unfolding before thee that ye be not taken unaware. It is said that ye shall be as ones prepared, for great changes shall come about upon the Earth.

For it is said, "Have no fear", for it is foreseen that the unlearned shall be filled with fear, and panic shall be their part. This, we of the Host of Light would prevent were it possible. While we, even of the forces of light, are somewhat subservient to man, for we are subject unto a greater law than Earth man. We are not within the bounds of

'Earth mans law'. We are the forerunners of freedom for all... all of the children of the cosmos.

* * * * *

LLL : For the time which is now come it might be said that the law is unjust. While these so saying are not prepared to make such judgement, for they are as blind as the mole, so to speak, as if they knew that which hast gone before, which now is the reaping.

These ones see not that which makes up the whole patterns of life, for this, each sees through his own lenses which are tinted with the many experiences of Earth existence. These, for the most part, are the subconscious memories which haunt them. For the most, these experiences are not clearly brought to the conscious mind for evaluation. This makes for admixture of fantasies and illusions, with no understanding of their origin.

That which we would give unto them in simple language is; that they have accrued much knowledge in aeons of past incarnations, which is not easily brought to remembrance. It is now time that the veil of remembrance be lifted. For this is there now a school prepared to receive them, for the purpose of enlightening these ones which have the will to awaken unto their heritage. This school is within the place which is designated as the Earth, yet it is not within the Earth. It is as a school of light... therein is no darkness. The ones so prepared shall be found and brought in by the ones which have the wisdom and authority for such as is necessary to be accomplished.

This is given herein as a very small reference unto this school, for it is not appropriate to go into detail at this point in time. By the time this portion hast found its way into the places of the populace there shall be a number of ones ready to be brought into this place of great learning, and revelation shall be as one of the greater parts. So be it that I shall speak further on this subject.

* * * * *

Sori Sori: While there are ones which know not of this school, I say unto ones which have the will to learn of the Law of life: "Wherein the mysteries are revealed, are ones prepared to be unto thee Master Teachers and Brothers from lands afar. These have come on thine behalf that ye be as ones prepared for a greater part." Blest are they which are found prepared to be brought in.

Now let us consider the conditions of the Earth plane on which ye abide at this time. It is of little value to give unto thee the fullness of this situation at this time, for ye have been warned in many ways and by thy scientists.

Now I shall speak fearlessly on a particular subject which ye know little, if anything, about. There is a place of great preponderance, wherein there are ones from out this galaxy which have volunteered to come into this place (the school), of which I have made, to give their wisdom and expertise that ye be as ones enlightened in the so-called "Mysteries."

It is said: "There are no mysteries after ye know", it is indeed true. So be it that the way is now made clear for the ones which are prepared to enter. The ones which are so prepared shall be as the

𝒮𝒮𝒮 of mine house, which is of light, and therein no darkness shall enter in.

It is expedient that each one be as free from superstition, hatred, and shame, for these ones which shall be brought in shall be found to be free from all darkness which is the result of persecution, bigotry, hatred... free from prejudice. (this is mans greatest cause of war)

As hast been written, and shall again be written, "none shall enter in without passport." What is a passport? Wherein shall I obtain this...this passport?

Let it be understood that thine little book (passport) which ye place within thine pocket will be of no value, for the one I speak of shall be as thine record taken from the Akasia. Know ye that thine record is clear unto these Master Teachers, which are masters of the Law of Life referred to in thine "Holy Books" of yesteryears. How think ye thine great records have been kept? Have ye been thoughtful of these which have been thine benefactors?

These which keep the records are well trained in such sciences as man of Earth hast not as yet dreamed. They are the ones which have brought forth thine every particle which hast been provided for thy benefit upon this planet. They have waited thine time when thou hast been as ones prepared to receive yet greater, fuller, knowledge... that which would bring thee into the 'Golden Age', which will indeed be golden. For there shall be no mistakes, no dogmas within this place of which I speak.

Ye may ask: Where is this place? The name? I say unto one and all: It is not known unto man of Earth by any name... it is sufficient that ye be brought in. Ye find not this place by mans means, or an ad in thine periodicals. Only thine record, if clear of any darkness, shall be sufficient unto thine entrance.

* * * * *

Sori Sori: The time is come when the Earth shall be delivered from her burden. Long has she labored in anguish. She hast given footing unto an ungrateful, rebellious generation, now it is foreseen that she shall be delivered of her burden.

For she hast carried within her womb a son, which hast come into his time of birthing. The Mother Earth shall be placed within another port; a place within the firmaments wherein she shall be as new born, wherein she shall be as a mother unto another generation. This generation shall be as the Sons of God. These shall honor her and be as ones worthy of her, for in her glory they shall rejoice with her in her new freedom.

Too, they shall be as guardians of the son which was sent forth from Mother Earths womb as she took flight through the firmaments. This son shall become the new moon spoken of aforehand. He shall be as a mature moon within the place which the Mother had occupied, for this shall be as the great part of change which shall be brought about within the heavenly spheres.

There are other movements which are taking place at this moment, which is of no account unto the sleeping populace of the earth at this period in time, yet there shall be a revelation revealed unto the ones which shall be as prepared to receive it. For first, there shall be ones placed in a place which is prepared for such as shall be given unto the ones prepared for such knowledge. These shall be trust-worth and as ones which shall go all the way with mine plan as it is revealed unto them. These shall be as the forerunners of great revelations. They shall be as the trumpeters, they shall be as the heralder of the new day, wherein there shall be no more war or sorrow... no more hatred and "black magic"; that shall be no more, for there shall be LIGHT, and there shall be peace and harmony for the ones which have cleansed themself and come unto the light which I Am.

There shall be a great light come forth within the radius of mans telescope, which shall enable him to see this light. This shall be as a mystery which shall confuse and confound him, for there shall be no accounting for this presence of such a light. Yet he shall find that there are greater and stranger things "out there" which he shall discover within the time of revelation, which is now at hand.

There shall come forth from the new school of revelation things which are beyond mans imagination; this shall upset all his theories and preconditioned ideas. This shall be the beginning of the "new day."

The time is upon man of Earth in which he shall see the past, including this day, as the dark age. He shall be as the little child which hast out grown his toys in such a short time. He shall wonder at his unknowing, his blindness, yet he shall take great joy in his new knowledge. So be it that I shall speak unto thee of greater things in the near time.

I now ask of thee, mine recorder, be ye at peace and poise that I might speak of things greater and more unto the understanding of the populace. I shall put it in terms which they can comprehend. So be it and selah.

* * * * *

THE EXODUS

Be ye as one which I have chosen for this part of this manuscript, for it is now time to place this information into the hands of the ones which are willing to learn. There is a multitude which are now beginning to stir. These shall be served, for the time for the sleepers is past. They which are found sleeping when the great sound is sent forth as the final call shall be as the traitor unto himself. He shall be as the one which hast thrown overboard his lifebelt when his boat is capsized. Let this word be as a warning unto these which have eyes to see and ears to hear.

It is our intention that all hear. Shall they be mindful of that which they hear? is the question. There shall be no slothfulness within the place prepared for to receive the ones which arise from their sleep and come forth as clean. These shall be as the ones to be brought out before the day of 'sorrow.' For it is with great wisdom and love that we of the Great and Mighty Council, hast a plan for the rescue of each and every living being which choose to be as one rescued.

This is but a poor expression of this magnificent plan of which we speak, for no word of mouth, nor pen, can express the glorious magnitude of our preparation for this exodus.

Let it be known that there is "a plan" in which great and glorious beings from far reaches of the cosmos have lent of themself that it, the plan, be brought to its perfection. There is no fear that it fail, for we are as one mind and purpose.

31

Mine part is that of going forth as one to awaken the sleeper, as to prepare him for to enter into the place of greater learning, wherein he might be of great help unto others in the time of stress, the time which we see as <u>great sorrow</u>. This is of great urgency, that man shall be given the opportunity to prepare himself for that which we see before him.

While he, man-mankind, is a myopic lot, he feels that he is within his place of present existence for a time, then he wonders that which shall be his lot. He fears for his future, or he claims to have no existence beyond his sojourn up to this his present planet. O, poor myopic wanderer whose time is come.

There are many which are now asking for light, and which are reaching for information such as 'we' have prepared for to give unto them. For this have we sent forth scribes and servants, sons and daughters, preparing the way for these who are alert and aware unto our call. These shall be as ones blest to answer this call sent forth.

Now it is sounded through the universe. We would have all, each one, come as one willing, prepared for the greater portion. While we see with greater vision, we know that all shall not be as we would have them be.

For these, the laggards, we have prepared a place wherein they may abide, in which they shall awaken and come into maturity. There are none overlooked, neglected, or forgotten, for we are of the light forces, sent of our source, the All Creator, the cause of our being, that 'His' creation be as made whole within its place and time.

There is no way in which we, of the Heavenly Host, can portray unto Earthman the perfection of our work of the divine plan. The magnitude of it can not be pictured within mortal mind... We would that it be possible. Let us be as a lamp unto thine feet, and a joy unto thine soul, for this have we entered into thine realm.

* * * * *

ꝋꝋꝋ : While there is a stir within the winds of truth, many a false prophet arises to proclaim the coming of the Lord. These are as ones which have but a crumb from the loaf, which think themself learned, yet know not that which they say is but the pall-parroted sayings.

There is no wisdom within them which preach from the places of man made sanctuaries, that they shall be gathered up with the Lord on the resurrection day. For it is a false doctrine which is not of the light or the 'Knowing Ones.'

There is a law concerning the coming, which is not of mans imagings. The way is set before man, yet many there be which know not that he is bound by the law by which all humankind is bound. Man is responsible unto this law, which is given unto him for his own welfare, his salvation, shall we say, using thy terminology. He ofttimes thinks of the man he so glibly speaks of as Jesus, as his 'God of deliverance', therefore he hast no responsibility to himself in his salvation. This is common unto man of Earth this day, therefore I shall not name them, neither shall I condemn them, for that is not mine mission at this time. I say "at this time", for it is now come that I have come again into the depth of darkness of a troubled darkened world for the purpose of arousing him from his deep sleep... his forgetfulness. I am within the realm of flesh and bone...

33

I am however not bound by flesh. I'm not limited in any manner whatso-ever, for I am the one which is of the light, sent of God the Father, which is above and beyond all other.

This is mine part at this time, to call forth a mighty host of light workers which know the laws of life... and these are with me as the Masters of the law... the eternal verities.

The dogmas of man-priests and the ones which set themself up as "wise and learned" are but the self-deluded, without wisdom/understanding of these laws of which I speak. It is now come when 'we' have been sent by 'The Creator' to bring these (laws) to the memory of the Earth-man.

For this hast he (man) labored in darkness, knowing not that he is bound. He hast bound himself, for he hast been as a rebel. He hast gone the long hard way around that he be not found and brought forth. He hast created that which hast been his own legirons.

For this do we now provide a plan for him to reinstate himself with the 'Light which never fails'. This I would have him understand; that there is a plan, conceived by the Sons of the Living God, within the place wherein sits the Mighty Christ Council, which is one with me, which are one with the purpose of this council; which is that of bringing light and deliverance unto a dark and sad world which stands on the brink of destruction.

Let it be understood that we are not impostors, we are in no need of self glory, neither fanfare. It is for the love which we share for mankind which hast lost its way, that we now draw close unto the Earth plane. We have heard the anguished cry of thine, as well as

34

Mother Earth, for the heavens proclaim thine stress and sorrow. Let it be a time of rejoicing, that help hast come to bring thee out of bondage.

We have prepared a plan which entails thine own cooperation. This plan is subject unto the "Great and Grand Plan", while there is one which applies to each man or woman which shall take his/her own responsibility for their action... every thought or deed.

It is said, ask of no <u>man</u> thine freedom, yet we see thee running hither asking of man, seeking advice, looking unto the 'wise' man for direction, when he too is bound by his own ignorance.

This plan of which I speak, includes a school which hast been referred to aforehand... set up within the near Earth, not upon it... for to prepare anyone, be he what-so-ever his color or sex/stature, might be found and brought in as he is prepared to enter in. He shall be as one prepared by cleansing himself of all hatred, all bigotry, condemnation of self as well as all others. He shall be purged of all guilt, and therein lies great wisdom, for it (guilt) is not found within this school of light. These truths shall be as the laws are taught/revealed.

These laws shall be revealed unto these ones which have proven themself trust-worth. None shall enter into this sacred place of revelation without sanction of the Great and Mighty Council.

This is the most sacred of places within the province of Earth. This place hast been long in preparation, yet it was finished at the proper time... loosely speaking of time. We are not limited by time, as ye know time, yet there are conditions which are part and parcel of mans will, his negativity, which does bring about certain results within the world of matter, which shall be recognized by the council; which is dealt with in love and wisdom.

There is much to consider while dealing with many factors of mans nature, his madness, hopes and fears, his rebellion and unknowing. These are all that he hast fashioned for himself, which is not of our nature, yet, we have the understanding which is given unto us for our experience through our sojourn through the cosmos, which enables us to understand the nature of all living things. Therefore we of the council are prepared to offer our expertise unto mankind that he be as one delivered out of bondage.

Now that it is come that this school of learning is established, and brought unto its resting place, it is offered unto each and every one as a free gift of mercy and love. We say unto thee, 'Children of Light', we welcome thee as brothers all, male and female. The conditions have been clearly set forth that there be no mistaken idea of said condition which must/shall be met before entrance is possible.

Bear in mind, this is a school of enlightenment, brought forth for mans eternal progress. This is not a fictional project, neither hast man imaged such grandeur or peace. Yea, peace is the overall attitude abiding therein.

Before man shall glimpse the glory of this place, which I have referred to as a school, he first has to give unto the source of his being recognition that he is a being brought forth through the Great Creator, as one with him (the source) made manifest in the material world... destined to go forth to know himself and his oneness with his source.

While in his new experiences he hast forgotten his source, for that he has wandered and wondered much from whence he came and wither he shall go. So be it he hast fallen from grace to become a lost being. He is lost, for his forgetfulness is his bound unto materiality. Knowing not his origin, he hast lost his way back unto his rightful place from which he went forth... forgetting his inheritance, his true birthright.

Now let it be understood that which is meant by these words, so inadequate to express such profound subjects are thine words. For this we have provided a means by which ye which hast proven thineself shall be blest to learn, to recall, to know that which hast been blanked from thine mind. Let it be, as ye are prepared so shall ye receive.

This is but the beginning of the revelations which is instore for thee. So be it I am the principal of this school; I am the founder, the executor of the plan which is now in operation. Be ye as one blest to be found prepared to enter therein.

*   *   *   *   *

This is mine project and gift to man of Earth, yet it is of the Father, creator of all, that we of the host are giving of our love and energy, for we are one, one with all creation.

What affects one part or planet, affects the whole. There is no division; all is bound together as one whole, within the Fathers over all plan. This we know, therefore, as we are one with the creator of all, we come in His name, or nature. This is His work made manifest through us, the 'Host' from afar.

* * * * *

There is but one truth; that of being one with the whole. When this is understood by mankind, each shall love one another as self and know themself to be one with the All... within the whole.

By the love and wisdom of the Mighty Council, we, thine benefactors, come into the Earth as the ones which see with greater vision. We are in a position to see that which hast gone before as we see that which ye call the present. The past too, we see as the now, for we stand at the crossroads of so-called time, therefore we see as ye can not.

There is much that ye shall learn before ye shall be prepared to call thineself "master" or "wise." There are ones of little knowledge which <u>think</u> they have come unto the place of great knowledge, which gives them license to teach that which they presumed to be truth. These have a great responsibility, for this is he held accountable... By the law which binds him is he held accountable.

* * * * *

Sori Sori: This is a time of great and sudden changes. This is but the beginning of the work which hast been allotted unto us of the Host, which have come into thine radius. As the work progresses ye shall come to know that we are about our part.

Bless this day. Give ye thanks that it is come, for it is the greatest play of force that hast been gathered upon and about this little orb since its existence. Let there be no doubt or confusion about this, for ye shall know that there is greater forces at work than ye Eartheans have or know about.

Be ye at attention, for it is at hand when ye shall stand in awe of that which ve see and learn. Ye shall be as ones which hast given no thought of such as shall be done or accomplished before thine eyes. However, thine eyes shall not behold the 'force', only the results thereof.

I say unto one and all: "keep thine position; be ye at peace and poise. Rest assured that ye are within the hands of the ones which are of the Father sent, which are thine benefactors". Be ye not so foolish as to run unto a neighbor and to ask his advice or opinion, for he knows not that which is being done.

However, ye need not expect that the plan be complete on the morrow or the day after. I say ye shall have another day in which to prepare thine self, for we have no intention to overpower thee or to catch thee napping. We say: "look... see... and learn to be ready for anything which is strange and new", for I say, there shall be the new which ye have no comprehension of. Be ye not fearful. Be ye at peace and poise. Panic not, for there shall be nothing to fear. Know ye that ye are safe within the light. Forget not that which we are saying unto thee, for thine own safety it is necessary to be as ones prepared. Be not so foolish as to overlook the instructions given, or ignore them. It might be thine undoing, which we do not desire.

By mine own hand have I given unto this, mine scribe and faithful servant, these words, which shall go forth as the fore-warning which is given for the benefit of each and every living being. We of the Host speak with one voice for the good of all humankind. So be it as the voice of the One Creator, the source of thine being.

* * * * *

Sori Sori: This shall be as the finish of this part of the little book which shall be put together. It shall be called "The White Star of the East". The name shall indicate the abiding place of the Host which hast come as one with me for to fulfill mine plan.

By the time it is prepared and into thine hands, there shall be great signs of the manifestation of this White Star. It shall be sighted and the astronomers shall marvel at such a phenomenon.

So be it that this work shall go forth as mine work. While the Host and I are of one mind, one intent, there is but one 'head', which I am. For that it is understood that I am the one which shall speak for the council at this period of time, for it is now come when the word shall be manifest.

Sananda

THE WHITE STAR OF THE EAST

Part II

Sori Sori: this day I say unto them which have a mind to learn, that there are ones which stand by which await them. These ones which await their (mans) preparation are as ones illumined, prepared to give unto them that which they have not learned within their halls of science.

We of the Host, have come from many galaxies to add our part unto that of our brother and compatriot, Sananda, for he hast formulated this great and marvelous plan which he hast now completed for the benefit of all which have the will, the mind, to come forth to partake of that which we are prepared to give unto them.

For this, we offer ourself that there be greater light within the world of man. That all darkness be no more, that there be peace within the place wherein mankind shall be placed when the hour strikes, for Mother Earth shall be evacuated.

This hast been referred to. Have ye, the ones which are now within the place wherein ye labor in bondage; do ye remember that which hast been said as a warning? Did ye take note? Are thou prepared to go forth as one prepared to enter into the school of which is prepared on behalf of the children of Earth?

I say, it is the greatest project which hast been brought into manifestation. Ye can not even imagine the magnitude of such as is brought forth in love and mercy, that there be light in the days of

41

darkness. This shall be as a continual effort until every living creature is removed from the planet upon which ye now have footing.

So be it I am one with the mighty Host, the Great and Grand Council. We speak with one voice, one intent; that of bringing freedom unto an awakening people. We will that all mankind awaken - So may it be. This is our mission, our intent.

* * * * *

These little sketches are given unto thee with the intent to awaken a thread of remembrance of thine many incarnations. It is not easy, for the thread is easily broken within the body of flesh, which hast the way of forgetfulness so impressed upon his psyche.

These threads too, are as links within the chains which bind thee unto the form of flesh. For flesh rebels against the release until there is a will so great, which shall be as the plan, for (before) his release is fulfilled.

The remembrance of time haunts the entity which picks up a thread of remembrance here and there. These remembrances ofttimes are the voice of thine guardian angels whispering unto thee. The angels are within reach of thine hearing, yea, they are part of thee. They are given unto knowing thine every thought, yet they know when to speak, to direct thee. They guard thy 'safe way' that ye stumble not, or fall by the way.

Yet, there are ones which rebel against these ones, ofttimes taking them down with thee, the rebellious ones... Then there is sorrow such as the entity has not imaged. These are "hells angels."

Hast thou heard of these? I say these are the greater of the pits of despair. Such torment!

Be ye apprised of such as is given unto mankind for his awakening, for this is it given. Think not ye are wise, ye which find but a crumb along thine long and tiresome journey "home."

* * * * *

Sori Sori: This day ye shall see the hand of God move. It is said, 'it shall move with precision', it is so! For this ye shall be prepared.

There shall be great light in the firmament and it shall be as no man hast seen. The astronomers shall be as amazed and bewildered at the appearance of this glorious sight. Some shall fear and be as ones confused, others shall run amuck, as animals gone mad. This is the time foretold, when the beast shall come out of the pit.

Now I have spoken unto thee of this as "the time to come", yet I now say unto thee, "the time is now, this day!" Open up thine eyes and see! I say, "open up thine eyes and see", for there are but few that are seeing.

For the most part, they which are asleep are not aware of the time of the "beast" (which) is upon thee. Have ye heard this expression? and where have ye heard it? Or have ye forgotten? I say unto thee, forget NOT these mine words, for to forget may be thine undoing.

We, the host, hast prepared a plan which is fulfilled for the good of all. Now, this day, we are announcing it that there shall be none caught off guard. We are one body of great learning and wisdom, which see with eyes which see, and a mind which is ONE with the

43

source of our being. We <u>know</u>, while man of Earth is the <u>thinker</u>, easily confused and frightened, thus he is the victim of many a false prophet which leads him astray. For his unknowing he is victimized!

I am now speaking on behalf of the Great and Mighty Council, that ye be as ones awakened unto that which is upon thee. These things are not revealed unto thee to frighten thee, yet it would be unlawful should we not warn thee.

Be ye not so foolish as to overlook the word which is fashioned for thine welfare, thine salvation! Yea, thine salvation! We shall make manifest our power upon the land, sea, and sky, that our presence be known.

Make no mistake, we, the Host, are sent of the source of thine being. Think ye that ye are not within, or under, the law and protection of one which hast been called "God"? Hast ye given thought of this protection, and from where comes it?

I say stop! Ponder well upon these words, for there is but little time to waste in idle thinking or wishing, neither running after soothsayers for advice, neither consulting the star charts. Ye shall find no comfort within either of these so-called masters or mediums. They too are in bondage.

We come that ye be as ones prepared for to be loosed of all bonds. It has been clearly stated aforehand that which is meant by "prepared". And again we shall repeat it that none can say; "We do not know what ye mean, prepare. How do I prepare? Where do I prepare?" We shall be explicit in our instructions, leaving nothing to bewilder thee or to confuse.

It is our intent to awaken thee, O man of Earth! I say, awaken and arise from thine long and deep sleep. For this we have sat long in council in the realm of light, wherein all things are seen and known, that ye be awakened and prepared to be brought out of bondage before the great day of sorrow.

Behold that which shall be made manifest before thee. This is what is meant when we say 'open thine eye that ye be not comforted by thine blindness', for ye shall be as one foolish to think ye might escape by closing the eye. I say unto one and all, "there is no escape." For it is our intent, our purpose, to awaken thee from thine slumber, thine lethargy, thine slothfulness.

Thine wickedness shall be as a great dragon to swallow thee up should ye choose the path of the dragon. He lies in wait. We would that ye see him for that which he is, and give him nothing which feeds his greed. Give him no footing within thine dwelling place. Nothing he can use against thee for he is a fearful taskmaster, jealous of his prey.

Be ye of a mind to learn of me, and comprehension shall be given unto thee. I am speaking for this great and mighty Council, for we speak as one, one voice in unison. We speak with one intent, that is for to bring thee out of bondage... to awaken thee unto thine rightful estate wherein is unlimited light and love... No more illusion.

* * * * *

Sori Sori: Wast it not said that there shall be greater floods, greater fires, greater sorrow. Is it not now upon thee? Hast ye noticed, or are thou yet asleep?

While ye hast slept there are a million people which are homeless this day from the ravages of quakes, fires, and aftermath. Hast it been a surprise unto thee? or hast thou been as one prepared? I hear ye ask, how can one be prepared for an earthquake?

Let it be said that ye, man of Earth, are the cause of the quakes. O, yes! O, yes indeed! It hast been said before, and shall be said again. For the Mother (Earth) hast rebelled, her spirit is crying out for relief. The time is come when she shall be put into another position wherein she shall have freedom from the cruelty, the hatred of man, which is the accumulation of that unrest which hast brought about the unbalancing within the interior of the body of the Earth, which hast effected the sister bodies of the solar system. Know ye this? Hast ye been apprised of this?

Let it be known that man of Earth hast been as the ones responsible for his part which he hast played in this "The Greatest Show on Earth." The "great drama" which he hast played in his time of sleep, in the dark.

Now, I hear the players which have come full cycle crying for relief, asking for light. So be it, it is now the hour when the "curtain" shall go up on this "Greatest Show on Earth." Art thou listening? Art thou present? Art thou aware of thine part which ye have played in this show? Remember, ye hast written thine own script.

Ye have forgotten thine lines... tis true. For this hast the great light appeared within the sky. Have ye seen it? or hast thou looked with thine seeing eye?

Be ye as one which shall awaken unto the mighty magnitude of the drama now being played out. Each and every player is in his proper place, and he stands in the dark of his own unknowing, his forgetfulness.

The hour strikes when ye, O man, shall see the curtain of this stage go up, and ye shall see that which hast been hidden from thee while ye have slept! This drama shall end in a burst of the greatest light that man hast ever experienced in his sojourn upon the Mother Earth. Then ye shall know the part which ye have played in the dark. Now it is come when the stage is set... The director calls "<u>alert</u>"... <u>prepare</u>... <u>ready</u>! Art thou ready?

Next...

Mine word unto thee this day is: Be ye alert... yet be ye not opinionated. For by any means what-so-ever shall ye be as ones enlightened on that which is yet to come forth from the realms of light.

It is said, "fear not" for ye which have the will to serve in truth/light shall find that ye are in good company, which have the intent to bring thee out of bondage.

Think not that ye are free! For we of the 'Host' see thee as a bound people in a very precarious position, created by thine ignorance of the law of the "One." Ye hast buried thine talents and gifts innumerable. These gift have come from the source of thine being, yea, by the grace of the one ye have called Father, God.

Rest assured that He, "It" hast a plan for all that is created alive. Let it be understood there is no end to life; it is eternal! Eternal I say! Ponder the joy of knowing, for this art we of the heights come that ye know the joy of everness.

* * * * *

For this do I speak as one with mine source. There shall appear in the east, a light such as man hast not seen. This shall cause great concern among the men of science, the superstitious, and these shall have great fear and some shall take their life, for their ignorance of this shall be as their own destruction.

This we would have them know; that there is nothing to fear. It is the "Star of Deliverance", sent of the "Father."

By the time of this lights appearance, ye of this knowledge shall be as one prepared to go forth as mine emissary unto them which are of a mind to follow this "White Star." These shall be as the ones to learn of the lighted ones which are ready to receive them.

It hast been said that there is a place prepared to receive them which have the will to serve the light for the good of all mankind. It is so written that there are ones which shall be frightened and rebel against the light which we of the Host bring for to light mans way in the time of great sorrow.

Too, we have said, fear not, for the 'Star' shall be thine deliverance. Be ye appraised of this and give ye thanks for thine knowing, for it shall be thine deliverance.

Cry not for the ones which rebel against the light, for they shall be as ones apart and separate from them which follow the Star. They shall be placed within their own environment, at and through their own vibratory rate, unto the likeness of themself.

Give ye heed unto that which is said unto thee, for it is for thine own sake we of the Host are revealing our self. Be ye not so foolish as to run hither and yon preaching fear or expounding thine opinions, for it is a great responsibility which could be thine downfall.

We would have thee prepared by and through us of the light before ye go out as an emissary. For this we have prepared a place for such learning; it is <u>as a place</u>, not an imagination or some idea of a fiction writer.

We are speaking simply in such a way that each and every one come to know that we ARE of good intent, and that is their deliverance.

So let it be.

* * * * *

Say unto them which will to serve in the light, that they are the ones which shall be given as they are prepared to receive. As they come forth they shall be given the choice of remaining among the people of the Earth, or going out into another environment. None are taken against their will.

Yet, it is foreseen that which these ones are, or shall be, prepared to do, for this we are given to see and know. Yet we are not prepared to take them against their will, for we do not break the law. Yea, I say, <u>we do not break the law</u>... war comes from such. We are not participants in breaking the laws of the cosmos.

Pattern thine laws after ours and there shall be only peace... and then ve shall be as acceptable unto the Christ Council, the federation of planets. The forces of darkness shall no more to be found about the Earth; then ye shall know freedom.

Bless this day, and be ye as ones willing to serve with us, the host of light, the ones which have come of our own will that all be set free, loosed from bondage. This is our intent, our mission.

While there are none which shall be given the bitter cup, there are the ones which are not acceptable unto us for/to enter into the higher realms of learning. It is by their own preparations that any one be accepted for the greater learning. When they are accepted, then we are as the ones prepared to take them as far as they are prepared to go.

While there are heights unlimited, we are not responsible for these ones which we know as neophytes. We give of our love and wisdom that they go all the way; that is, as far as their strength and desire allows.

* * * * *

Sori Sori: There is a time in which the cycles are at an end... finished. Then there are sudden appearances which betokens the new. It is now come when the great and grand cycle hast ended, in which this phase of the work of bringing out the children of light. This hast been referred to as the "resurrection", the day of the "deliverance".

Now it is called or referred to by some as the "lift off". This is the time for the ones which have the will to listen/learn, and a will to be lifted into another dimension of time and space.

This is as new unto some which are beginning to stir or see that which is going on round about them. While there are ones which will to close the eye and not look or see, they shall deny our existence, for they fear that they be found out in their wickedness. These are the ones which shall be caught off guard; they shall be found wanting.

Now let us speak of the ones which are prepared to receive us, and of us. These shall be gathered together into the place wherein they shall be sorted, each unto his own likeness, for like draws unto its self its likeness. None shall be out of place, for each shall have a number, a color, a musical note such as ye have not heard or imagined. These beings shall be as ones dealt with in wisdom, love, and great compassion. Wherein they go shall be determined by number, color, and that musical note.

Each hast created his tone and color, for he shall emit from himself such light as speaks for himself, it's self. There shall be no guess work, for we of the Light Force shall know each entity, as we are prepared for that service unto all life by the Father-Mother God, which hast given unto us the privilege of serving mankind in such a capacity.

This is but a very short and indeed a crude, simple, report of our placement and part which is given unto us to play in this the "Greatest Show on Earth". Yea, this is the last great drama to be played in the 'dark', for we come that there be light! So shall it be. For this have we given of our love and wisdom.

Ye know not the magnitude of our work at this time, yet it is said: "All things shall be revealed unto them which are prepared to go all the way with me." I have stood at the door long, and called: "Come home! Come home mine children". Hast thou heard mine call? Hast thou moved thine feet? opened thine eye or thine heart unto me? Or hast thou sought out mans council/advice and consolation in the time of suffering and sorrow?

O, mighty wanderers on the periphery of time and space, wanderers of the night, I say, awaken unto mine call. Arouse thine self and answer me when I speak unto thee, for I shall speak as one which shall make mineself understood when ye open up thine mind, heart, and will to hear me. I shall give unto thee that which ye are prepared to receive.

Ye shall not be deceived, neither shall ye seek out the soothsayers, for that is the foolishness of the fools which put the foot into their trap.

Be ye as ones to seek the light which I Am, for I am sent of mine Father that ye be brought out of darkness, 'bondage'. That ye be eternally Free. So let it be as the Father hast willed.

Sori Sori: This is the time of the revelations of old, fulfilling. That which was spoken in the days of the great plagues of the Earth are as naught today, for it is a new day, a new time. New promises, new fulfillings. Ye of this "New Day" are under a new dispensation. The Firmaments declare a <u>New Order</u> which shall be given within the heavens; 'a promise of thine freedom'.

It is written that a new thing shall be done, that which ye have not imagined. This shall be manifest within thine sky as a gleaming white star. It shall move from east to west at the speed of a star, yet it shall have the appearance of the sun. It shall cast its radiance upon all the Earth as no other heavenly body.

There shall be great confusion within the men of science, for they which have thought themself wise shall be as lost for to explain this wonder, for they have not foreseen the coming of such a body of light.

Now that it is so recorded, let them which discover this white star take note that it is so recorded within this day of so-called miracles. For there shall come from the heavens a great cloud of ships which have no wings, no 'smoke towers', no fumes, no poison. These shall be as the promise of the ages past. "<u>The heavens shall declare the glory of God</u>". So be it! Amen.

Let thine eyes be made to see, thine heart to rejoice. Sing ye a glad song and be ye blest to receive him which is come, for thine deliverance is he come. Then ye shall see and know that ye are not alone, that thine deliverance is nigh. For this is it said; "Be ye faithful in little things, and ye shall be given in greater measure".

Ye have been given bit by bit as ye could bear. Now it is come when ye shall open up thine eyes and comprehend that which ye see. That which ye see shall be by no means of Earth's 'going on' or manifestation. No machinery, no armor, shall be as necessary for thine protection against this, the Army of the Lord of Hosts, for it is for thine deliverance. Let no fear be within thee, for to fear shall be thine undoing.

It is clearly written, there shall be one come to deliver thee out of bondage... Remember? Wast it not so written in thine 'holy book': "as with a cloud"? Let it be as within a cloud, for it shall be as such. Soft... noiseless... floating majestically... beautiful to behold.

Ye, man of Earth, ye shall leave thine house and go forth in love, and honor him, the Master of this great armada from the heavens. Great shall be the cries of joy; He is come... The Lord of Hosts... He is come!... HE IS COME! Praise Him the Lord God... The Lord of the Host is come!!!!

Be ye blest this day is come, when man shall see him face to face. So be it, it is so recorded that ye be prepared to receive him.

* * * * *

Sori Sori: The day of decision is come. It is given unto the host to know that which is expedient to reveal unto mankind at any given point in time. So be it that there hast been sent unto the Earth plane at these times, ones which have been prepared to give forth that which is, or was, propitious at that time, or for that cycle. Much of the 'word' given at these 'times' have been held for this day when the children of this age have sufficiently awakened that they comprehend that which hast been given through these ones which I have given the part of communing with me.

I say, I deny none which-so-over are prepared to speak mine words in toto, in truth, and in the manner in which I would them give it forth. While it is seen that many go so far, then they find that they give of their energy unto their wants and desires of the mundane world, forgetting that I am the spirit of truth, the sure and safe way to all knowledge, which is the fulfilling of all man needs for his ascension into the greater, fuller, life, wherein there is no want or bondage.

For this hast many been given to record mine sayings, mine word, which has been recorded upon the record of the great screen of time, which fades not away. These words of truth which I speak, which are so recorded for all time, are available unto each one which is so prepared to see and understand.

It is said, there is no mystery other than thine unknowing... 'tis so. For this is it written that ye shall "first seek the light, and all things shall be revealed unto thee". The meaning is simple, clear unto all. Where there is a will to learn of the light which I Am, the spirit in which ye, one and all, live and have thine being, ye shall be as one come alive and know that which ye are, 'born of light', for all substance, including thine flesh body, is of this substance of light.

Man is given unto thinking, which is his unknowing. "As he thinks, so he becomes", hast been as another cliche, which hast no meaning unto the initiate. The one which is the knower hast the knowledge of himself and the mission upon the Earth plane. He has the knowledge of the elements and how to use the power of speech for the good of all. He gives not of himself unto the forces of darkness. He goes about as the one given his freedom. As he moves among men in bondage, he sends forth radiance which is felt by the one so quickened to receive it.

While there are so very many which are walking about as robots, unknowing, knowing not of their own being, no understanding of that which sustains them. These are as ones which have not partaken of the "Cup of Life", the joy of being! These are the sleepers. These are the ones which shall be shaken until they do awaken, for it is so written it shall be, for the darkness shall no longer consume mine people.

I Am the Light of the world. It is so declared in the eternal light of the heavens.

* * * * *

Sori Sori: This shall be mine testimony unto all people of all nations of the planet Earth. Let it be recorded as I speak it. There shall be no inaccuracies, for I shall be as the author and editor.

It is now come when there shall go forth from the heavens, a light, blinding unto the sleepers which are not as ones prepared for such as this. There shall be a great fear, this resulting from their stubbornness and rebellion, for it hast been foretold in many ways. And the ones which are caught off guard shall quake with fear... some shall give unto themself the bitter cup (even suicide). This is not of the light, not of the hosts of light, it is of their own rebellion and bigotry.

For this I would have them heed, listen, and comprehend that which is come upon them. This is the day of sifting and sorting. The ones which refuse to stand up and be counted shall be placed in a place wherein they shall wait another "day", another cycle of light, wherein they shall be prepared for to go into greater light realms. For the darkness shall weigh heavily upon them which refuse that which we of the host bring unto them at this time.

This, the White Star of the East, shall go before the host now, as of the day so long ago when the child was born in Bethlehem. Wast it not foretold? or have ye heard?

Now, this is but the reminder of the days ahead when many strange things shall be shown unto thee, man of Earth. This is <u>only a small reminder</u>... wait not to see. Wait not for the climax of this The Greatest Show on Earth. For the first acts are now being played behind the curtain, the curtain of unbelief, unknowing, while ye have danced to the pipers tune.

This is the day of soberness. It is said: "lay aside thine foolish way and take up thine shield of protection", for it shall be fortuned unto the sober one to hear and heed this last call, which shall go forth in the greatest time which man hast been privileged to be on the Earth plane.

Give unto me thine hand and heart, thine will, to go all the way with the light which is made manifest within the heavens as the Star of the East. Let thine opinions and prejudiceness be no more... thine bigotry shall be thine downfall. These characteristics of man shall be as chains about thine neck.

This is that which I would that ye take unto thine own self and consider, for thine own sake let it be. For I say unto one and all: Ye have no concourse into the realms of light save through this means which is now being presented unto thee. No man can, or shall, decree other wise.

So be it that this is mine testimony, and the truth is proven in thine experiences when the great day dawns upon the eastern horizon, as the light which shall bring thee deliverance from thine bondage. So be it.

* * * * *

Sori Sori: Upon the precepts of the light of the Great Creator of all beginnings are our works and plans formulated. This is that which we of the Christ Council would have thee understand, for it is now seen that the time is come for thee to be further learned in the things/ways, of progression of "man". For man, as ye, is sleeping within flesh. He hast little knowledge of his being, his reality, his eternal reality.

Now, it is known amongst us which make up this mighty Council of Light, that it is now time that ye awaken unto thine true identity. For this it is necessary that ye be brought into the place wherein is a place for thee, that ye might go all the way into the light that never fails. This hast been given unto thee in many ways, which ye have not comprehended. While it is so planned, so shall it be.

Now that it is most expedient that ye be prepared for the greater part, there are many to assist thee in that which ye shall be allotted to do. For there is a place wherein ye shall see and hear, and know that which ye see. Then ye shall return unto them fully prepared, capable of conveying unto them that which is truth, for there are few which have the full knowledge of that which they proclaim/expound as truth.

It is foreseen that these with whom ye have knowledge of, these which have asked for truth, shall be as ones blest of thee that ye shall return unto them in the manner which is given unto thee, as ye shall return unto them as new. And they shall be as ones to bear witness of these mine words.

I have said, blest are they which holds fast unto me, for they find me a friend and benefactor. I forsake not that one which I call forth as mine chosen, yet the one call shall answer me and follow mine precepts. He shall be blest to know mine voice, mine touch, and I shall walk and talk with him until the time is appropriate to bring him in.

Let this be known, (this mine word unto thee at this hour), at the time of thine departure, not before, for it would be misunderstood. This is not 'our' intent to mystify them, for there is no mystery except thine unknowing. While it is a time of sifting and sorting, there is timing in this, all things are timed by events. Is it not said many times; "As Ye Are Prepared So Shall Ye Receive". So it is... So it is... So shall it be.

Be ye as one now prepared to enter into this place prepared to receive thee, and ye shall not fear or be alone. For there shall be many to receive thee and ye shall know such joy as ye have never known. Such things which have mystified thee shall be made clear unto thee; then ye shall go forth as one qualified to give unto them as ye have learned... this is, unto the ones which are prepared to receive such learning.

I say <u>learning</u>, for learning is quite different from <u>information</u>. We are not simply informers, we are at the place wherein we are, that man of Earth learn of his heritage and accept it as his precious gift of the Father, which ye call God... thine Source of Being.

This is the day ye have long awaited as thine awakening, when thine eyes shall be opened unto the glory of the heavens. There shall be nothing hidden; all shall be revealed in truth, light.

Blest are they which are prepared to enter into the place which is now ready to receive thee. So be it and selah.

* * * * *

"When it is come when mine star is seen in the east,

it shall be a sign unto man that I Am come unto them,

for their deliverance is nigh".

* * * * *

Recorded by Sister Thedra

www.ingramcontent.com/pod-product-compliance
Lightning Source LLC
Chambersburg PA
CBHW070759050426
42452CB00012B/2407

*9 7 8 1 7 3 6 3 4 1 8 2 7 *